A Year of Mindfulness

a year of mindfulness

A 52-Week Guided Journal to Cultivate Peace and Presence

Jennifer Raye

ROCKRIDGE
PRESS

Cover Design: Bethany Robertson & Matt Girard
Interior Design: Matt Girard
Art Producer: Sue Bischofberger
Editor: Crystal Nero
Production Manager: Riley Hoffman
Production Editor: Melissa Edeburn
Illustrations © Bethany Robertson, 2019

ISBN: Print 978-1-64152-749-1

Printed in Canada

To my mom for encouraging my love of writing, and to my dad for teaching me that I can do anything I set my mind and heart to.

This Journal Belongs to:

_____

The thought manifests as the word;
The word manifests as the deed;
The deed develops into habit;
And habit hardens into character.
So watch the thought and its ways
with care, And let it spring from love
Born out of concern for all beings.

~ THE BUDDHA

Introduction

IMAGINE YOUR MIND AS A WIDE-OPEN SKY that can hold all experience. This empty space remains undisturbed as clouds pass. Mindfulness teaches us to access the clarity and freedom of this open sky.

In many ways, mindfulness is radical and revolutionary. It is a living practice that asks us to see things clearly beyond biases and judgment. The English translation of mindfulness comes from the Pali word *sati*, which means "bare attention" or "remembering." *Sati* originates in Buddhism, but similar contemplative teachings can be found in other traditions.

Mindfulness promises to wake us up. It can help strengthen our basic goodness, guide us to a healthier and wiser life, assist us in relationships with ourselves and others, and can lead to deep inner fulfillment. Its methods and philosophies can be applied universally regardless of background.

In our fast-paced world with the constant pull toward distraction, mindfulness can teach us how to slow down and be present. While formal meditation is an important part of the practice, mindfulness can also be used during everyday moments. It can become a regular companion on our path, like an old friend or a home base. We can return to it regardless of the clouds in the sky. With practice, mindful awareness is available every moment. Ultimately, it's simple: Just pause and notice your experience with loving attention.

When we develop awareness, acceptance, and kindness toward all aspects of our experience we can see that we have a natural radiance, just like the wide-open sky. I'm delighted to share these meaningful practices with you. I know firsthand the boundless possibilities that mindfulness offers. It has personally enabled me to cultivate understanding and peace, which has helped me in countless times of struggle.

I'm deeply grateful to my teachers and those who have influenced me on this journey. Many of the prompts and practices in this journal were inspired by the teachers you'll find mentioned at the end of this book. I certainly have more to learn from this profound practice, but it's my intention to offer a small piece of the path to you here.

This journal focuses on four themes of mindfulness practice: *Center Your Body, Explore Your Mind, Take Care, and Celebrate and Appreciate.* Within these pages you'll find practical exercises you can easily weave into your day. Feel free to start at the beginning or skip around. It's my hope that this form of everyday mindfulness will aid you in finding greater ease, releasing unskillful behaviors, and strengthening your connection to the planet and all beings. Turn to this journal daily and use the inquiries to learn about mindfulness and explore yourself. Mindfulness happens before interpretation, in a place of relaxed concentration. I encourage you to spend a few moments in quiet contemplation with each exercise before filtering the information through your thinking mind and writing your responses.

I've also put together a collection of resources to support you, including some audio meditations to accompany the book, which you can find at www.jenniferraye.com/mindfulness. Remember mindfulness has to be learned. It takes practice, dedication, and patience. Stay with it and be consistent. I know you can do it!

Congratulations on taking this step toward a more mindful life. May you be well, may you be at peace, and may you know your true nature.

Center Your Body

Awareness of the body is an essential ingredient when developing mindfulness. Whether you're driving to work, doing the laundry, or sitting in meditation, the body is always available.

When you pay attention to the body you become more centered and grounded. Mindfulness of the body reduces preoccupation with thinking, shows you how your body, mind, and heart are deeply connected, and helps you understand impermanence and change.

If you're new to mindfulness, paying attention to your body may be a pleasant discovery, but it can also be a challenge! During the seated meditations, make the practice work for you. Listen to your body and adjust your position if you feel uncomfortable. Stick with it and you'll discover that a world of insight, subtlety, and wisdom awaits you.

Explore Your Mind

You probably don't pause and examine your thoughts very often. Mindfulness helps you slow down and notice what you're thinking.

When you pay attention to the mind, you'll most likely discover an endless stream of quickly changing thoughts rising and falling at any given moment. It can be quite surprising to realize this inner narrator is constantly offering plans, preferences, ideas, and memories!

When you observe your thoughts, you have the opportunity to rest in the silence and space between thoughts. And you can choose which thoughts you want to nurture and which thoughts you want to let go.

Take Care

As you pay attention to your inner world, you'll probably notice your inner critic and negative mind states. This negativity is rooted in feelings of unworthiness, insecurity, and fear, causing a disconnection with ourselves, others, and the world around us. It's normal to have times of difficulty, anxiety, and struggle. You can't always change your circumstances, but you can work with how you relate to them.

An attitude of love, kindness, connection, and compassion counteracts negativity and is an important companion when practicing mindfulness. Practicing self-care and kindness softens your heart and teaches you how to hold yourself, your life, and others with gentleness in every moment.

Celebrate & Appreciate

Every day you have the opportunity to sow the seeds of gratitude and joy. When you take the time to consider the simple moments, you'll find there's so much to celebrate and appreciate!

Gratitude is a practice that helps you be present with whole-hearted attention. Studies show that taking note of what you're thankful for leads to more happiness. It could be a kind word from a loved one, the feeling of sunshine on your face, or finding a deep appreciation for your inner strength and beauty. Whatever the cause for celebration, this practice can help you access contentment and joy.

Center Your Body

WEEK 1   DATE _____

1. Find a seat and relax. Breathe slowly through your nose. As you inhale and exhale notice how the breath affects your body. Feel your body expand and contract. Where do you feel the breath?

_____

_____

_____

2. Center your attention on your body. Notice how it is full of sensations. Some sensations may be stronger than others. Is there one area speaking to you right now?

_____

_____

_____

3. We do many daily activities on autopilot. Today, slowly make your bed. Notice all of the little moments; the tucking of rumpled corners, the fluffing of pillows. What's it like to notice the ordinary moments?

_____

_____

_____

4. What do you feel in your body right now?

_____

_____

_____

5. Set a timer for 10 minutes. Lie on your back and widen your awareness to include your whole body. Notice where you're feeling tense. Invite the tension to release by softening. Record any insights on the lines that follow.

_____

_____

_____

6. During your next meal thoroughly smell and see the food you're eating. Observe the colors and aromas of the food. What did you notice?

_____

_____

_____

7. Go for a walk today and strive to be present. With every step feel the placement of each foot on the ground. What was it like to completely feel your body walking?

_____

_____

_____

Explore Your Mind

WEEK 2

DATE_____

1. Find a comfortable position and close your eyes. Set a timer for 10 minutes. Acknowledge every time you notice a thought. When the timer goes off, reflect: Did the thoughts seem fixed or did they come and go?

_____

_____

_____

2. Next time you're brushing your teeth, aim to be present. Take note of when you start thinking. It may seem like a small practice, but the mind wants to jump all over the place! What's it like to pay attention to this single task?

_____

_____

_____

3. Next time you feel bored, pause and notice something in your environment. Take note of its details. What's its color or shape? Is it moving or still? How does this activity of paying attention change your boredom?

_____

_____

_____

4. What are you thinking right now?

_____

_____

_____

5. The mind is like a storyteller. Sometimes these stories are helpful and sometimes they're not. Is there a story you've been telling yourself lately? What is it? Could there be another way to look at it?

_____

_____

_____

6. Evaluate your overall thoughts so far today. Have they been positive? Negative? How?

_____

_____

_____

_____

7. When you first wake up tomorrow notice your thoughts. Are they active or slow? How does that feel?

_____

_____

_____

If you start to experience impatience, confusion, or disconnection during these practices, that's okay. Return to the practice without judgment. The purpose of practice is not to attain some perfect state. The essence of mindfulness is the willingness to let go and start again.

Take Care

WEEK 3

DATE_____

1. Next time you're in front of a mirror, take a few extra moments to smile at yourself with genuine care. This may feel silly at first or trigger other emotions and feelings. That's okay. Let yourself feel. What happened?

_____

_____

_____

2. When life gets busy it's easy to lose connection with your internal experience. Spending some time on self-inquiry is an act of self-care. Ask yourself: How am I doing right now?

_____

_____

_____

3. Take note of the sensations you feel. When you notice pain or discomfort offer love to that area. Release tension and send the thought "May you be well" to the discomfort. Did you notice any change in the discomfort or your thoughts about the discomfort?

_____

_____

_____

4. Find a comfortable position and relax. For the next 10 breaths silently repeat to yourself: "May I be well." Feel the power of the words. Record your experience.

_____

_____

_____

5. Reflect on your basic desire for wellness or happiness. This primary urge exists within all humans. Feel the simple beauty of that idea. Record your thoughts and feelings below.

_____

_____

_____

6. What is one special thing you can do for yourself this week?

_____

_____

7. Next time you're cooking a meal for others, think of the people you're cooking for. Send them loving-kindness as you cook. Imagine them happy and at peace. Reflect below.

_____

_____

_____

Celebrate & Appreciate

WEEK 4   DATE_____

1. Call to mind a time when someone helped you. Invite a feeling of thankfulness into your body, heart, and mind. Why were you grateful for that help? What difference did it make?

_____

_____

_____

_____

2. Find an object in nature. Choose something small but special. Notice its simple beauty and observe its shape, texture, and color. What do you appreciate about this object?

_____

_____

_____

_____

3. Next time you sit down for a meal, pause and imagine all of the living beings involved in getting the food to your plate. Offer thanks for the nourishment. Who did you thank?

_____

_____

_____

_____

4. Reflect on your strengths. Pick one strength and think of the ways it's helped you. Why do you think it's a strength? How have you used it to help yourself and others?

_____

_____

_____

5. Think of one well-known person who has made the world a better place. Reflect on the qualities they possess that you admire. Who did you choose? Why?

_____

_____

_____

6. When this week did you feel your best? Why?

_____

_____

_____

7. Write a list of five things that bring you joy and delight.

_____

_____

_____

_____

_____

Focusing on sensation is a great way to bring your attention to the present moment and cultivate mindfulness. Take a moment and notice sensations in your body. Below, make a list of what each sensation feels like right now.

_____

_____

_____

_____

_____

_____

_____

_____

_____

_____

_____

_____

_____

_____

_____

_____

_____

_____

Attention is the
beginning of devotion.

~ MARY OLIVER

Center Your Body

WEEK 5

DATE_____

1. Lie on your back with your legs bent. Place one hand on your chest and one on your belly. For 10 breaths watch the movement of your hands. Does one hand move more as you breathe?

_____

_____

_____

2. Attend to the sensations in your body. Do you feel pain or discomfort? Instead of thinking about why the pain exists or how to fix it, simply experience the sensation. What does it feel like?

_____

_____

_____

3. Do some stretching or yoga for the next 20 minutes. Observe the sensations that occur during the movements. As you stretch ask yourself: Where am I feeling this? Is it strong? Does it feel warm? Does it change?

_____

_____

_____

4. Where in your body do you feel grounded right now?

_____

_____

_____

_____

5. Next time you're in the shower aim to be totally present. Take note when you start thinking and return to the present moment. How was it to pay attention so closely?

_____

_____

_____

_____

6. How does your body feel when you're stressed?

_____

_____

_____

_____

7. Set a timer for 10 minutes. Lie on your back, widen your awareness, and listen to the sounds that come and go. Was it difficult to keep your attention on the sounds?

_____

_____

_____

Explore Your Mind

WEEK 6

DATE _____

1. Set a timer for 10 minutes. Relax your body and notice your breath. On every inhale silently say to yourself: "I am here." After the 10 minutes record any thoughts or feelings.

_____

_____

_____

_____

2. Set a timer for 10 minutes. Acknowledge when you notice a thought. Whenever you catch yourself getting distracted, bring your attention back to observing your thoughts. What repetitive thoughts did you have?

_____

_____

_____

_____

3. LOOK BACK to week 5 #2. Pay attention to discomfort in your body again. Do you notice your mind wanting to label the sensation as good or bad? When you're feeling discomfort what happens in your mind?

_____

_____

_____

4. Remember a time recently when you experienced anger. Bring the whole event into your mind's eye. How does thinking about this event feel in your body?

_____

_____

_____

5. Bring your attention to your toes by wiggling them. Then hold your toes very still. Can you still feel them using only your mind?

_____

_____

_____

6. Notice what you're thinking and feeling right now. If it had a color, what color would it be?

_____

_____

_____

7. Do some light stretching. Include movements that you like and others you don't. How did your mind react when doing the stretches that you like versus the ones you don't?

_____

_____

_____

Take Care

WEEK 7   DATE_____

1. What is one special thing you can do for a loved one this week?

_____

_____

_____

2. In this practice, aim to befriend yourself. For the next 10 minutes say to yourself: "May I be safe," and "May I be free from fear." As you slowly repeat this aspiration, feel the meaning and impact of the words on your body and heart. Did any feelings of unworthiness arise?

_____

_____

_____

_____

3. Next time you notice that you're upset, pause and allow yourself to feel. Hold the feeling with care. Repeat to yourself: "I accept this," without trying to change the feeling. Was it challenging to accept that you were upset?

_____

_____

_____

_____

4. Choose a simple loving phrase or mantra to use today. As you go through your day repeat this phrase to yourself as a way to care for yourself. What mantra did you choose?

_____

_____

_____

5. Place your awareness on the physical location of the heart. Notice any feelings that arise. What does the heart feel like right now? Is it tight? Soft? Is it easy or hard to connect with?

_____

_____

_____

6. Bring your attention to a time when you did something good. What did you recall?

_____

_____

_____

7. Find something that makes you laugh. Maybe it's a favorite movie, a book, or memory of a loved one. Let go of any seriousness and make yourself laugh. Reflect below.

_____

_____

_____

Celebrate & Appreciate

WEEK 8   DATE_____

1. How can you celebrate and appreciate this week?

_____

_____

_____

_____

2. Think of a time when it would have been easy to lie or hurt someone and you chose not to. Feel the warmth and delight of that realization. Reflect below.

_____

_____

_____

_____

3. Reflect on your success. Pick something you've accomplished in your life that you're proud of and let yourself appreciate it. Recognizing your positive attributes helps you access a happiness that was hidden until now. What did you choose? Why?

_____

_____

_____

_____

_____

4. Spend some time organizing your home today. As you pick up take a moment to appreciate the items you find. Perhaps they've helped you in some way. How does it feel to appreciate the small things?

_____

_____

_____

5. What are you grateful for today?

_____

_____

_____

6. What is one thing you like about yourself right now?

_____

_____

_____

7. Next time you're with someone you love, suggest that you both spend a moment telling the other person one thing you like about them. What did they say about you? What did you say about them?

_____

_____

_____

_____

Mindfulness helps us see the mind clearly. Use the next five minutes to write down everything that comes to you. Don't censor your thoughts. Get everything you're thinking onto the paper.

By cultivating an unconditional and accepting presence, we are no longer battling against ourselves, keeping our wild and imperfect self in a cage of judgment and mistrust. Instead, we are discovering the freedom of becoming authentic and fully alive.

~ TARA BRACH

Center Your Body

WEEK 9   DATE_____

1. Sit comfortably and relax. For 10 cycles of breath, bring your attention to the exhale. Where in your body do you feel the exhale? Do you feel it in your belly? Your ribs? Somewhere else?

_____

_____

_____

2. Turn on your favorite music, let go, and dance! In addition to being fun, dance helps memory, mood, and cognitive function. When you're finished dancing, pause and ask yourself: "What's happening in my body right now?"

_____

_____

_____

3. Close your eyes and turn your awareness to the inside of your mouth. Observe the sensations on your lips, your tongue, and the insides of your cheeks. Notice any taste present. What do you feel?

_____

_____

_____

_____

4. Soften your eyes and sense the inside and outside of your ears. Don't let your eyes lead the way. Can you feel the individual parts of the ears?

_____

_____

_____

5. Pay attention to your hands today whenever you think of it. What did you notice?

_____

_____

_____

6. Lie on a blanket and bring your attention to the back of your body. Scan it slowly from the head down to the toes. Which parts are touching the blanket? Which are not?

_____

_____

_____

7. Sit comfortably and relax. For 10 cycles of breath, bring your attention to the inhale. Where in your body do you feel the inhale? Do you feel it in your belly? Your ribs? Somewhere else?

_____

_____

_____

Explore Your Mind

WEEK 10

DATE_____

1. Aim to clear your mind for the next 10 minutes. Invite your thoughts to slow down. Imagine your brain activity becoming quieter with every breath. Are there thoughts that are difficult to quiet?

_____

_____

_____

_____

2. Next time you're driving or are in transit, observe when you start thinking or planning. For the remainder of your trip can you concentrate only on what's happening right now?

_____

_____

_____

_____

3. Clean up your space mindfully. You can choose a large area like a whole room in your house, or a small area like one desk drawer. What thoughts, feelings, and memories arose?

_____

_____

_____

_____

4. Set a timer for 10 minutes and close your eyes. Observe your thoughts. Afterward do you feel a little more relaxed? At ease? In tune?

_____

_____

_____

5. Some habits of mind are skillful and lead to awareness, and some are unskillful and lead to disconnection. Name three unskillful and three skillful thoughts. What would it be like to nurture the skillful and let go of the unskillful?

_____

_____

_____

6. Think of something you're worried about. Is there a story your mind is telling that is making the worry worse?

_____

_____

_____

7. Are your thoughts pleasant, unpleasant, or neutral right now?

_____

_____

_____

Take Care

WEEK 11

DATE_____

1. You probably know everything changes. Life is a continuous series of gain and loss, pleasure and pain. Do you think there are inner qualities beyond these ups and downs? What are these inner qualities for you?

_____

_____

_____

_____

2. **LOOK BACK** to week 7 #5. Notice the heart now. How is it different from last time?

_____

_____

_____

3. One of the ways we block ourselves from experiencing joy is through feeding guilt. Do you sometimes feel guilty when you experience something good in your life? Reflect on the lines that follow.

_____

_____

_____

_____

4. What caring act can you do today for yourself?

_____

_____

_____

5. Choose one small behavior you want to stop and a healthy habit you can replace it with. Pick something easy and specific. Record the behavior and your habit below.

_____

_____

_____

6. What evening ritual would nourish you and help you prepare for a restful sleep? Some yoga? Meditation or prayer? A warm bath? Journaling? Deep breathing?

_____

_____

_____

7. Do something special when you're getting ready that makes you feel good. It could be putting on a piece of clothing, a little makeup, or a beautiful scent. Enjoy!

_____

_____

_____

Celebrate & Appreciate

WEEK 12   DATE_____

1. Reflect on your motivation to practice mindfulness through this journal. The quality of your intention will seep into the level of benefit you receive. What is your deepest wish for these practices?

_____

_____

_____

2. Gratitude helps us re-orient our perspective so that we feel more positivity in our lives. At the end of the day ask yourself: What did I accomplish today? Be grateful for what you discover.

_____

_____

_____

3. Write a list of five people who have supported and loved you in some way.

_____

_____

_____

_____

4. Before you get out of bed tomorrow take a moment to appreciate the coming day. You could think of activities, small opportunities, and connections you'll have. What are you looking forward to?

_____

_____

_____

5. What are some reasons you like the weather today?

_____

_____

_____

6. Explore your thoughts and ask yourself: What do I truly need (that I already have) to be happy?

_____

_____

_____

7. Your senses are how you perceive the world. Appreciate what your senses do for you. Imagine your life without the ability to hear, see, smell, taste, and touch. How would life be different?

_____

_____

_____

Choosing stress over calm can become a habit. Negative mind states are a normal response to difficulty, but are you feeding these negative mind states too often? Get some insight by coloring the circles below.

I REGULARLY FEEL...

What did you discover? If you found some stress circles colored in, how might you build more calm into your life?

Be faithful in small things
because it is in them that
your strength lies.

~ MOTHER THERESA

Center Your Body

WEEK 13   DATE _____

1. Find a comfortable position and focus on your breath. Don't try to change it. Are the spaces between breaths long or short? Are these spaces the same length or different?

_____

_____

_____

_____

2. Next time you eat, slow down and focus on chewing. Taste every bite. This is not only a practice of mindfulness, it will also help your digestion. How did you feel after your meal?

_____

_____

_____

_____

3. Dress comfortably and go to a natural place outside. Sit or lie down and connect to the environment. What can you touch? See? Hear? Smell? Taste? Are some senses easier to identify than others?

_____

_____

_____

_____

4. How does your body feel when you're peaceful and calm?

_____

_____

_____

_____

5. Pay attention to your feet on the ground today whenever you remember. What did you notice?

_____

_____

_____

_____

6. Within your body you can sense elemental qualities. Today, focus on the earth element. Notice the parts of your body that feel firm and solid. Do they help you feel grounded? How do you experience the earth element?

_____

_____

_____

_____

7. What is one loving act you can do for your body today?

_____

_____

_____

WEEK 14   DATE_____

1. Clinging and attachment are common states of mind. We think we know what we need to be happy and we project that desire onto a particular outcome or person. But the mind is not always right. Describe a time when you wanted something, only to discover it was a good thing you didn't get it.

_____

_____

_____

_____

2. Is there anything you're trying to force to happen in your life right now? What kinds of thoughts are present when you push?

_____

_____

_____

_____

3. Set a timer for 15 minutes. Soften your eyes and watch as thoughts come and go. Every time you detect a thought, notice if it's pleasant, unpleasant, or neutral. What did you discover?

_____

_____

_____

_____

4. How is your mind right now?

_____

_____

_____

5. Pay full attention to a single body part for the next five minutes. Notice how your mind stopped thinking when you were focused. What was that like?

_____

_____

_____

6. Mindfulness can also involve the dreaming mind. Do you remember your dreams?

_____

_____

_____

7. Choose a small object to keep in your pocket today. Every time you notice it, pause and acknowledge what you're thinking. What were your thoughts like?

_____

_____

_____

_____

It's common when starting a new endeavor to have a lot of expectations. This can lead you away from the purpose of mindfulness, which is to be fully here now. If you've been wrapped up in expectations and struggling because you're not getting results, return to your heartfelt intention. Remember, mindfulness takes time.

Take Care

WEEK 15

1. In the Buddhist tradition, the nature of the heart is sometimes described as being obscured by dust. What do you do that creates this barrier? What could you do to brush away the dust?

_____

_____

_____

2. Tension and fatigue can easily build up in the eyes. Rub your hands together and cup your eyes with your palms. Soften and feel your nerves relax. How did that feel?

_____

_____

_____

3. Draw a hot bath for yourself. Light candles, and add your favorite essential oil or bath salts. Invite tension in your body to melt. Enjoy. How did it feel to grant yourself this gift?

_____

_____

_____

4. Spend 20 minutes cleaning out your kitchen drawers. What you bring into your kitchen is what you ultimately end up putting into your body! Clear out the gunk. Ask yourself: What is no longer serving me?

_____

_____

_____

_____

5. What caring act can you do today for someone else?

_____

_____

_____

_____

6. Self-care is an important part of leading a life of ease. Take a moment and contemplate: What happens when I don't take care of myself?

_____

_____

_____

_____

7. Choose one positive word for today.

_____

Celebrate & Appreciate

WEEK 16

DATE_____

1. Choose a houseplant or a plant in your yard. Strengthen your connection with the natural world by simply treating it with care. Check in with your plant regularly and respond to its needs. Reflect on what this experience is like for you.

_____

_____

_____

_____

2. Bring to mind something that made you laugh recently. Let it enter your mind and body. Feel any warmth associated with the thought. What was the memory? How did it feel?

_____

_____

_____

_____

3. Write a list of five people you deeply care about.

_____

_____

_____

_____

_____

4. Think of someone in your life that you sometimes have conflict with. Can you think of one positive quality they possess? What is it?

_____

_____

_____

5. How can you celebrate and appreciate someone in your life this week?

_____

_____

_____

6. What is one thing you appreciate about your environment right now?

_____

_____

_____

7. Think of a happy memory from your childhood. It doesn't have to be a big memory, just something simple. Let any feelings arise. What did you remember?

_____

_____

_____

_____

Make yourself a cup of tea. For the next 10 to 20 minutes invite yourself to wholly experience drinking tea. Appreciate all aspects of the experience. Notice how the tea makes you feel. Cultivate gratitude as you enjoy every sip.

_____

_____

_____

_____

_____

_____

_____

_____

_____

_____

_____

_____

_____

_____

_____

_____

_____

Out of love, our path can lead us to learn to use our gifts to heal and serve, to create peace around us, to honor the sacred in life, to bless whatever we encounter, and to wish all beings well.

~ JACK KORNFIELD

Center Your Body

WEEK 17   DATE_____

1. Your body is sacred and beautiful. How could you remind yourself of this today? Perhaps through your use of clothing, jewelry, a favorite scent, or scarf?

_____

_____

_____

_____

2. Become still and imagine your breath radiating out from a center. Where in your body do you feel this first moment of breath? Is it in the belly? The middle or upper chest? Somewhere else?

_____

_____

_____

_____

3. Get out into nature and take your shoes and socks off. Open to your natural surroundings. Did you feel any exchange of energy between you and the natural world? What was it like?

_____

_____

_____

_____

4. Where in your body do you feel tension right now?

_____

_____

_____

5. Turn to the water element in your body. Consider how the body is mostly made of water. Is there anywhere in your body that you sense moisture and fluidity? Where do you feel the water element?

_____

_____

_____

6. Let out a big sigh. How did that feel?

_____

_____

_____

7. Set a timer for 10 minutes. Find your seat. Feel your body sinking and grounding. Imagine that your lower body is growing roots down into the earth. What was that like?

_____

_____

_____

_____

Explore Your Mind

WEEK 18

DATE_____

1. Let your attention travel down to the earth and then let it flow upward to the sky and the space around you. Shift your awareness between these two poles a few times. How do you feel now?

_____

_____

_____

_____

2. Tonight as you fall asleep, count your breaths. With every exhale, mentally count "one," "two," and so on. Let your mind rest and just count. What number did you get to?

_____

_____

_____

_____

3. Place a lit candle in front of you. Soften your eyes and focus your attention on the flame. When you notice your mind wander draw your attention back to the flame. Be steady but not rigid. Can you balance your effort?

_____

_____

4. Find an animal or insect near you to observe. Write about it in detail.

_____

_____

_____

5. Name one current thought that is pleasant, one that is unpleasant, and one that is neutral.

_____

_____

_____

6. LOOK BACK to week 10 #5. Have you been able to work with the unskillful thoughts and nurture the skillful ones? If not, why? Remember, be kind to yourself no matter what you discover.

_____

_____

_____

7. Imagine your mind as a wide-open sky. Let thoughts arise and pass. Can you allow your mind to rest in the clear and open space of the sky?

_____

_____

_____

Take Care

WEEK 19   DATE_____

1. What is one special thing you can do for your home this week?

_____

_____

_____

2. Choose one caring word for today.

_____

3. Brainstorm one cause you deeply care about. How can you help and get more involved?

_____

_____

_____

4. Go to bed early tonight. Slow down, turn off technology, and enjoy some quiet time. Record how you feel the next day.

_____

_____

_____

_____

5. Think of someone you have neutral feelings toward. This could be someone you see often, but don't know well. Picture this person and reflect on their basic wish to be happy. Silently repeat: "May you be well." Record your experience.

_____

_____

_____

_____

6. We all carry around physical and emotional baggage that weighs us down. Make a list of things you're ready to let go of.

_____

_____

_____

_____

7. We can gain confidence in the practices of kindness and care by recognizing the benefits it brings. Meditate on the simple positive effects of self-love. What came to you?

_____

_____

_____

_____

Celebrate & Appreciate

WEEK 20   DATE_____

1. How can you celebrate and appreciate someone at work this week?

_____
_____
_____
_____

2. Find a comfortable position either sitting or lying down. For the next 10 breaths, imagine you are inhaling peace and exhaling stress. How do you feel now?

_____
_____
_____
_____

3. Think about the people in your life who have supported you. In particular, have you had a significant mentor or teacher in your life at any point? What was it like to receive guidance from them?

_____
_____
_____
_____

4. Go out into nature and listen to the sounds. What sounds attracted you?

_____

_____

_____

5. What positive changes have happened in your life in the last year?

_____

_____

_____

6. Remember your first job or another important workday that was challenging. Recall how you may have felt scared or nervous. What is at least one way you did a great job that day?

_____

_____

_____

7. Look back at your week and ask yourself: Was there something challenging that you managed really well? Explore on the lines that follow.

_____

_____

_____

_____

Stand with your feet about hip width apart. Keep your feet and legs stable and gently bend your knees. Twist your torso side to side. Allow your arms to swing. Breathe through your nostrils and coordinate your breathing with the movement. Infuse your body with energy and vitality.

KNOWING THAT YOU LOVE THE EARTH CHANGES YOU,
ACTIVATES YOU TO DEFEND AND PROTECT AND
CELEBRATE. BUT WHEN YOU FEEL THAT THE EARTH
LOVES YOU IN RETURN, THAT FEELING TRANSFORMS
THE RELATIONSHIP FROM A ONE-WAY STREET INTO
A SACRED BOND.

~ ROBIN WALL KIMMERER

Center Your Body

WEEK 21   DATE_____

1. Focus your attention on the breath. Notice its rhythm and don't try to change it in any way. Count the length: How long is the inhale? How long is the exhale?

_____

_____

_____

2. Your body is intimately connected to the natural world and the seasonal cycles. Observe what season you're currently in and ask yourself: How can I attune to this seasonal rhythm?

_____

_____

_____

3. Next time you prepare a meal check in with your body. You get to decide how you feel through what you consume. Do you want to feel warmer? Cooler? Heavier? Lighter? What did you discover?

_____

_____

_____

_____

4. Where in your body do you feel at ease right now?

5. What would help you let go and land in your body right now?

6. Consider the fire element by noticing cold and hot in your body. Can you discern if the front of the body is warmer or cooler than the back? What about the interior versus the exterior? Or the top versus the bottom?

7. How does your body feel when you're anxious or nervous?

Explore Your Mind

WEEK 22

DATE_____

1. Sometimes the mind holds onto pain. Neglected emotional memories can lead to difficulty, and processing these events leads to better health outcomes. Write freely about a distressing time in your past. Explore the details and your emotions.

_____

_____

_____

2. Collect your attention. Breathe. Observe thoughts coming and going for 10 minutes. When you look directly at your thoughts what happens? Do they continue? Or do they change in some way?

_____

_____

_____

3. Set a timer to go off occasionally today. When it goes off, spend one minute closing your eyes and expanding your awareness. Relax and allow everything to be as it is. How did that affect your day?

_____

_____

_____

_____

4. Go into nature and find an object to observe. Describe the object in detail using all of your senses. Observe images, feelings, and memories that emerge. Record below.

_____

_____

_____

5. Next time you notice a pleasant thought observe how it feels in your body. What did you discover?

_____

_____

_____

6. Go outside and watch the clouds. Let your mind wander. Observe the clouds passing through the sky. Examine carefully. How are your thoughts like the clouds?

_____

_____

_____

7. Your mind is a powerful force. Tonight, set your intention to remember your dreams. Write down what you remember first thing in the morning. Did you remember anything?

_____

_____

_____

Beginner's mind is a very important concept when practicing mindfulness. So forget what you know and be open to surprise and what arises naturally. It's okay to be a beginner. In fact, it's helpful!

Take Care

WEEK 23   DATE_____

1. What is one special thing you can do at work this week?

_____

_____

_____

_____

2. LOOK BACK to week 3 #4. Set a timer for 15 minutes. Repeat the practice by sending yourself kindness. Then consider how all beings everywhere wish for wellness, too. Extend your care to all beings. Was it easier or more difficult for you to extend your wishes outward rather than inward?

_____

_____

_____

3. In conversation with a friend or loved one, practice mindful listening. Observe when you start thinking about what you're going to say next, and strive to be present instead. Do you think that changed the conversation?

_____

_____

_____

_____

4. Choose soothing sounds to listen to today. You could choose nature sounds or meditative music. What other sounds did you hear today? How were they different from the soothing sounds?

_____

_____

_____

5. Commit a random act of kindness today. This act doesn't have to be big. Find someone and lend a helping hand. Cultivate a sense of care for this person. What happened?

_____

_____

_____

6. Use an essential oil like lavender diluted in coconut or sesame oil. Mindfully rub the oil on your feet before bed. Enjoy the scent and the practice of self-care.

_____

_____

_____

7. Choose one inspiring word for today.

_____

When using practices that build loving-kindness, it's normal for feelings of disconnection or sadness to sometimes arise. If that happens for you, remember there is no need to change. Rather, practice acceptance and send care to the disconnection. You are exactly where you need to be.

Celebrate & Appreciate

WEEK 24

DATE _____

1. Think back to a time you immersed yourself in study and practice of some sort. Examine how the experience of deep study affected you. What did you gain from that experience?

_____

_____

_____

_____

2. Think of something that made you smile today, or if you're doing this practice in the morning, something that made you smile yesterday. What was it?

_____

_____

_____

_____

3. Take a moment and think of your favorite place. Picture this place and let yourself feel gratitude. Where did you choose?

_____

_____

_____

_____

4. Make a list of qualities you admire in others. Take time to appreciate these qualities.

_____

_____

_____

5. Find one place in your body that you appreciate. Let yourself enjoy it. Maybe it's because of how it looks, or maybe it's because it does something for you. What did you choose? Why?

_____

_____

_____

6. How could you find greater meaning in your life? What do you most deeply yearn for beyond material goods, fame and praise, pleasure and comfort?

_____

_____

_____

7. What are some things you like about your job or work?

_____

_____

_____

What kinds of thoughts do you want to have this coming week? Pick a word from the list below or think of your own:

Kind

Abundant

Joyful

Simple

Purposeful

Loving

Spiritual

Open

Playful

Calm

Generous

Connected

Clear

Adventurous

Free

Faithful

*We must be willing to let go of
the life we have planned, so as to
accept the life that is waiting for us.*

~ JOSEPH CAMPBELL

Center Your Body

WEEK 25   DATE _____

1. What is one way you can get your body moving today?

_____

_____

_____

_____

2. Stand and reach your arms up on the inhale. Exhale, bend forward and reach down to the earth. Then roll your spine back up to standing. Practice five times and modify the movement if needed. Feel the air in your lungs and the movements in your body. What sensations do you feel?

_____

_____

_____

_____

3. Begin by relaxing and closing your eyes. Draw your attention to your breath. Notice the texture of your breath. Is it rough? Smooth? Does it speed up or slow down at certain points?

_____

_____

_____

_____

4. Where in your body do you feel warmth right now?

_____

_____

_____

5. Inspect a natural food like a blueberry, almond, or cranberry with all of your senses. Roll it around in your fingers, squish it, taste it. Notice how it looks, feels, smells, and tastes. Describe.

_____

_____

_____

6. Are you holding tension in your shoulders and upper back? Pay attention today whenever you think of it. What did you notice?

_____

_____

_____

7. Next time you're getting groceries, notice the vegetables you don't usually choose. Go home with something new you're attracted to. What did you choose? Why?

_____

_____

_____

Explore Your Mind

WEEK 26

DATE _____

1. Next time you're getting ready for work aim to be present. Take note when you start thinking. What are your thoughts like?

_____

_____

_____

2. Go for a 20-minute walk and aim to stay present in your body. Set a timer to chime at five-minute intervals. Every time the timer goes off, ask yourself: "What's happening with my mind now?"

_____

_____

_____

3. Aversion is a mind state that makes you want to move away from what you don't like. But sometimes you can't run away. Next time you need to do something you dislike, notice aversion and experiment with cultivating more acceptance. What was that like?

_____

_____

_____

_____

4. Next time you notice an unpleasant thought take note of how it feels in your body. What did you uncover?

_____

_____

_____

5. Become quiet and relax your body and mind for 10 minutes. Visualize your mind as a muddy pool. With every breath the pool becomes clearer and the sediment settles. How do you feel now?

_____

_____

_____

6. What is the overall emotional flavor of your thoughts right now? Sweet? Bitter? Bland? Spicy?

_____

_____

_____

7. Set a timer for 10 minutes. Relax, close your eyes, and notice the space after the inhale and after the exhale. What happens to your thoughts in these spaces between breaths?

_____

_____

_____

WEEK 27   DATE _____

1. What is one supportive thing you can do for yourself out in nature this week?

_____

_____

_____

_____

2. Choose one empowering word for today.

_____

3. This evening, take a moment and mentally rehearse tomorrow. Infuse the day with moments of warmth, happiness, and kindness. Is there a way to imagine your day going smoothly?

_____

_____

_____

_____

4. Settle into your body and take a moment to assess your internal weather. How are you doing right now?

_____

_____

_____

_____

5. Caring for others can be a way to care for ourselves. On the lines that follow, make a plan to volunteer in your community. How could you contribute?

_____

_____

_____

_____

6. Sit in a relaxed way and enjoy a few deep breaths. Bring into your mind's eye someone you know who is struggling. Silently repeat a phase of kindness: "May you be at peace." Feel the wish in your body, mind, and heart.

_____

_____

_____

_____

7. Give yourself some extra love. Use a scrub on your skin, clip your nails, massage your face and body. As you clean and brighten your body, aim to clear your mind. How do you feel now?

_____

_____

_____

_____

_____

Doubt in the form of constant questioning can get in the way of mindfulness. Some doubt is healthy; it allows you to investigate and discover the merits of practice for yourself. But doubt can also halt progress. If you've been questioning your abilities, return to your heartfelt intention and let it feed your determination and perseverance. You're doing great!

Celebrate & Appreciate

WEEK 28   DATE_____

1. Think of a friend or family member you love. Write them a short note and tell them how you feel.

_____

_____

_____

_____

2. Contemplate your life history. What positive changes have occurred? Write about one way you've grown.

_____

_____

_____

_____

3. List a few friends whom you consider wise and good-hearted. Allow yourself to feel thankful for these people in your life. What do you appreciate about them?

_____

_____

_____

_____

4. Think of something that made you laugh so far this week. What was it?

_____

_____

_____

5. Set an alarm to go off at regular times throughout your day. Every time the alarm goes off pause and send yourself or another person wishes of love and care. Share your experience here.

_____

_____

_____

6. What are three basic needs you have met every day? Elaborate on why these things make you grateful. Get specific and descriptive.

_____

_____

_____

7. Life is imperfect. That doesn't make it any less beautiful. Make a list of imperfect people, things, or experiences in your life that are still beautiful to you.

_____

_____

_____

Is there someone you're ready to reconcile with? Write a note below and explain how you feel. This exercise can be for you, or you can share the note with the other person.

_____

_____

_____

_____

_____

_____

_____

_____

_____

_____

_____

_____

_____

_____

_____

_____

_____

_____

_____

_____

Vulnerability is the birthplace of love, belonging, joy, courage, empathy, and creativity. It is the source of hope, empathy, accountability, and authenticity. If we want greater clarity in our purpose, or deeper and more meaningful spiritual lives, vulnerability is the path.

~ Brené Brown

Center Your Body

WEEK 29   DATE_____

1. Find a comfortable position and focus on your breath entering and exiting your body. Allow the breath to come and go without manipulation. Do you notice any parts of the breath that seem to get caught or that feel stuck?

_____

_____

_____

_____

2. Are you holding tension in your belly? Pay attention to your abdomen today whenever you think of it. Soften and let go. What did you notice?

_____

_____

_____

_____

3. Reach your arms up to the sky and take a deep inhale. As you release your arms let out a big exhale through your mouth. How did that feel?

_____

_____

_____

_____

4. Think of a decision you're currently trying to make. Close your eyes and relax. Feel your body. Ask yourself: Does this choice bring me energy? Does it drain me? How does this choice feel in my gut?

_____

_____

_____

5. Where in your body do you feel cold right now?

_____

_____

_____

6. Next time you notice you're upset, consider your breath. How has it changed?

_____

_____

_____

7. Find a comfortable position and relax. Feel your body settle and become grounded. What feels stable amid all that changes?

_____

_____

_____

_____

Explore Your Mind

WEEK 30

DATE_____

1. Next time you're about to eat your favorite food, pause. As you take your first bite, observe closely the pleasant experience, What is it that you like? Is it the taste? The texture? What happens after the first few bites? Does the experience change somehow?

_____

_____

_____

2. Set a timer for 15 minutes. Close or soften your eyes. Notice thoughts coming and going without holding on. Notice how you think. Do you think in words? Images? Sounds? Some other way?

_____

_____

_____

3. Lie down and rest your attention on your body. As physical sensations arise notice how they affect your mind. Do you try to hold onto pleasant sensations? Push away unpleasant sensations? Zone out when there's no sensation?

_____

_____

_____

4. Mindfulness can be translated as "remembering." Close your eyes and settle your thoughts for 15 minutes. Aim to "remember" presence when your mind deviates. Simply notice this act of remembering.

---

5. Next time you notice you're spaced out and not paying attention, observe how you feel in your body. What did you find?

---

6. One of the foundational causes of suffering is misperception. Think of something you're having a hard time with right now. Ask yourself: Is my perception accurate?

---

7. Is there a person or memory you've been thinking about lately? Why do you think that is?

Our habit-driven minds can be tricky to work with! It's okay if some practices are challenging, but it's also important that you find practices that lighten you up. If you find a particular prompt really enjoyable, feel free to return to it. Connect with your internal wisdom and do what works for you.

Take Care

WEEK 31

1. Clean out some of your closet today. Let go of items you no longer use and make a pile to give to charity. Was it hard to let go? How does it feel to create space?

_____

_____

_____

2. Choose a place in the world that is struggling due to natural disaster or political or social turmoil. Imagine the people affected. Allow yourself to feel. Spend five minutes meditating on suffering while slowly repeating a phrase of kindness such as: "May you be free from suffering." Reflect in the space that follows.

_____

_____

_____

3. Happiness is not a finite resource. In fact, when we share it, it grows! Next time you see someone who is experiencing joy or good fortune, take a moment to feel happy for them. Let happiness radiate outward. There is no limit. Describe your experience.

_____

_____

_____

4. Take 15 minutes today to withdraw and rest. Lie down on your back. Use an eye pillow or wrap a scarf around your eyes. Relax your body and breath deeply. How do you feel now?

_____

_____

_____

5. Think of a time when you did something generous. It could be big or small. Is there a time you can remember? What was it?

_____

_____

_____

6. Ask yourself: How can I act and speak honorably and nobly today?

_____

_____

_____

7. What worked well in your life in the last week? What didn't work well?

_____

_____

_____

_____

Celebrate & Appreciate

WEEK 32

DATE _____

1. Make time today for an activity or hobby you enjoy. What did you choose?

_____

_____

_____

_____

2. Call to mind a specific time when you learned something from a difficult situation. Invite a feeling of gratitude into your body, heart, and mind. Why are you thankful for what you learned? How did it shape you?

_____

_____

_____

_____

3. Make a list of five things that help you feel grounded and stable.

_____

_____

_____

_____

_____

4. Think of a material item you love and cultivate gratitude for what this item brings you. What did you choose?

_____

_____

_____

5. Name a book that had a positive impact on you. How did it shape and affect you?

_____

_____

_____

6. Think of a person in your life who is sometimes difficult. Then, reflect on a positive quality they possess. How did that change how you see them?

_____

_____

_____

7. When this week have you felt the most calm? Why?

_____

_____

_____

_____

_____

Create a small sacred space for yourself. It could be a corner of a room, or an area on your desk. Make it personal and beautiful. Decorate it with special objects that remind you of happiness, peace, and belonging.

Everything in our lives has the potential to wake us up or to put us to sleep. Allowing it to awaken us is up to us.

~ PEMA CHÖDRÖN

Center Your Body

WEEK 33

DATE _____

1. Breathe like you're filling a vase. Feel your belly fill, then your mid-chest, and finally your upper chest. Then gently release in the opposite direction—upper chest, then mid-chest and belly. Don't force. Stay present. How did that feel?

_____

_____

_____

_____

2. How does your body feel when you're fatigued?

_____

_____

_____

3. Set a timer for 10 minutes and practice walking meditation. Find a small area to walk and synchronize your breath with the movement of your legs. Stay present. Record any insights.

_____

_____

_____

_____

_____

4. For the next 10 breaths, sigh with an "ah" sound on the exhale. How do you feel now?

_____

_____

_____

5. Close your eyes and notice your whole body. How do you know where your body is in space without moving?

_____

_____

_____

6. Stand upright and side bend. Bring your awareness to the sensations during the movement. As you stretch, ask yourself: Where am I feeling this? Is there a difference from side to side?

_____

_____

_____

7. Rub your feet for the next five minutes while repeating to yourself: "I appreciate my body." How is it for you to care for your body?

_____

_____

_____

Explore Your Mind

WEEK 34

DATE_____

1. Relax in open space for 15 minutes. When you notice something arise in your mind, silently label it and let it go. For example: "planning," "judging," "listening," "irritation," "buzzing," "hot," "cold," "past," "future," and so on. Reflect.

_____

_____

_____

_____

2. Observe your thoughts. Do they have an emotional tone? Are they anxious? Angry? Joyful? Remember: It's not important for your mind to be a certain way. Thoughts are only visitors.

_____

_____

_____

_____

3. **LOOK BACK** to week 30 #3. Do the exercise again and this time, ask yourself: What would it be like to not prefer certain sensations over others?

_____

_____

_____

_____

4. Recount a time recently when you experienced fear. Bring the entire event to mind. How does thinking about it feel in your body?

_____

_____

_____

5. Imagine yourself without any of the roles you identify with. Imagine you have a mind that doesn't hold onto identity. Who are you now?

_____

_____

_____

6. It's easy to have preferences for certain mind states. Are there mind states you label as wrong or right? What would it be like to let go of the judgment?

_____

_____

_____

7. Set a timer for 10 minutes. Relax your body and notice your breath. Notice the rising of thought and emotion. Can you separate the two? Record the differences.

_____

_____

_____

Take Care

WEEK 35   DATE_____

1. Oftentimes we use our speech to spread gossip instead of using it to spread joy, understanding, and compassion. How can you care for yourself and others today with your speech?

_____

_____

_____

_____

2. What is one memorable thing you can do for your family this week?

_____

_____

_____

_____

3. Think of a difficult aspect of yourself. Place a hand on your heart or belly and reflect on your basic wish to be happy. Silently repeat: "May I accept myself." Record your experience.

_____

_____

_____

_____

_____

4. Choose one uplifting word for today.

_____

5. Set a timer for 15 minutes. Think of all the living beings that make up the world. Use a phrase of care like: "May all beings be well." Radiate this care in front, behind, above, below, and side to side. Describe your experience.

_____

_____

_____

_____

6. Is there something in your life right now that is filling your heart up? What is it?

_____

_____

_____

_____

7. Take 30 minutes today to read a book for fun. Which book did you choose?

_____

_____

_____

_____

Remember to allow yourself to feel. Compassion is the practice of connecting to your tender heart and the pain you sometimes feel. Contacting your feelings will help you respond skillfully and open to a deeper level of compassionate connection with others.

Celebrate & Appreciate

WEEK 36   DATE _____

1. Take a moment to appreciate the fact that you have the opportunity to create your day. Plant some seeds of intention on the lines that follow. What would you like to create?

_____

_____

_____

2. Contemplate an area of your life that makes you feel awake and vital. What is it?

_____

_____

_____

3. Next time you sit down with your family or members of your household, propose that you each offer a few words of gratitude. What did people share?

_____

_____

_____

_____

_____

_____

4. What is one thing you appreciate about your family?

_____

_____

_____

5. Think of something that helped you let go of stress and feeling overwhelmed this week. What was it?

_____

_____

_____

6. Go for a run, walk, or bike ride. As you move, observe and truly appreciate the natural world all around you. What did you notice?

_____

_____

_____

7. Contemplate the privilege you have. Take a moment to appreciate how it's helped you in certain areas of your life. What did you discover?

_____

_____

_____

_____

Using coconut, sesame, or massage oil, give yourself a short loving massage. Use gentle pressure and pay extra attention to your joints and any areas that are calling to you.

Your hand opens and closes, opens and closes. If it were always a fist or always stretched open, you would be paralyzed. Your deepest presence is in every small contracting and expanding, the two as beautifully balanced and coordinated as birds' wings.

~ RUMI

Center Your Body

WEEK 37   DATE _____

1. Turn to the air element. Experience the qualities of lightness and motion by moving your body and then stopping. Can you sense the movement and stillness of the air? What's it like?

_____

_____

_____

_____

2. What is one way you can love your body today?

_____

_____

_____

_____

3. Be mindful of your body parts for 10 minutes; visualize muscle, skin, tendon, bone, fluids, and organs. Get specific. Notice the full nature of your body. Did you find any parts unpleasant? Do those parts also have a helpful, or even beautiful, function?

_____

_____

_____

_____

4. Where in your body do you feel openness right now?

_____

_____

_____

5. Set a timer for 10 minutes. Stand with your knees gently bent, spine lifted, and shoulders relaxed. Close or soften your eyes. Practice standing meditation by observing sensations. How was this different from a seated meditation?

_____

_____

_____

6. Enjoy a big breath. Relax your belly and shoulders. How did that feel?

_____

_____

_____

7. Stand up and shake it out. Swing your arms, move your legs, wiggle your fingers, and let go! Keep going until you feel complete. How do you feel now?

_____

_____

_____

There's no rush. If you find an exercise hard to connect with, notice if you're experiencing any anxiety about time. Let go of grasping. Relax and let the answers appear to you in their own way. Give yourself this moment.

Explore Your Mind

WEEK 38   DATE_____

1. Are you feeling insecure in any area of your life right now? Do you think there's another way to look at it?

_____

_____

_____

2. Next time your mind is feeling sluggish or sleepy, get up and arouse energy by moving your body. Did this help to counter-act the slowness in your mind?

_____

_____

_____

3. Are you engaging with anxiety in your life right now? Fear and anxiety can block true wisdom and joy. They make you worry about the future, or some imagined circumstance, and cause you to miss the present moment. Can you open your mind to include your anxiety while staying here and now?

_____

_____

_____

_____

4. Take a seat and soften your eyes. Breathe and relax your body. For 10 minutes, notice the thoughts that come and go. Ask yourself: Who am I? Who am I beyond my thoughts?

_____

_____

_____

5. What mind state would you say is strongest for you right now?

_____

_____

_____

6. Next time you're eating breakfast try to be present. Monitor when you start thinking and instead draw your full attention to the task at hand. Was it difficult? Easy?

_____

_____

_____

7. Sometimes when we slow down it's easier to be mindful. Choose a simple activity. Next time you do the activity, really focus and go slower than usual. What did you notice?

_____

_____

_____

Take Care

WEEK 39   DATE_____

1. What is one supportive thing you can do for youself this week?

_____

_____

_____

2. Letting go of resentment and practicing forgiveness can be a very powerful act of self-care. Forgiveness is not condoning or denying what happened. It's a quality of the heart in which we release the grip of negativity. What are you ready to forgive?

_____

_____

_____

3. Your body language, facial expressions, words, and actions have a very real impact on how people perceive you and therefore the kind of day you have. Reflect on how the world around you responds to your mood.

_____

_____

_____

_____

_____

4. Close your eyes and engage your curiosity. What would feed your being right now?

_____

_____

_____

5. A big part of practicing mindfulness is reversing our constant need for more. One way we can do this is through the practice of generosity. Think of one way you can be generous today. Write about it.

_____

_____

_____

6. What is one small health habit you could strengthen or start today?

_____

_____

_____

7. In every moment you can strengthen a sense of separation or connection. Think of a person you have difficulty with. Be gentle, allow all feelings, and silently send a phrase of care to this person. What was your experience?

_____

_____

_____

Celebrate & Appreciate

WEEK 40   DATE_____

1. Remember a time when you dedicated yourself fully to something and you did it out of pure love. What was it? How did that experience change you?

_____

_____

_____

_____

2. Describe one way in which suffering has sofened your heart.

_____

_____

_____

_____

3. Fall asleep tonight with wholesome thoughts. Make a determined intention to let go of worries and instead think of what's working in your life. What can you think of?

_____

_____

_____

_____

_____

_____

4. Write a list of five things that make you feel whole and healthy.

_____

_____

_____

_____

_____

5. Recall a time when you learned a new way of seeing things you hadn't considered before. Explore how this new perspective changed you.

_____

_____

_____

_____

6. Think of someone in your life who inspires you with their passion, purpose, and direction. What is it you find enlivening?

_____

_____

_____

_____

7. When this week did you feel your strongest? Why?

_____

_____

_____

Brainstorm some positive affirmations on the lines that follow. Get creative. Do you want to feel whole? Accomplished? Enthusiastic? Strong? Magical? Overflowing? Create some sticky notes with the affirmations you chose and post them where you'll see them as little reminders.

I WANT TO FEEL . . .

May I meet this
moment fully.
May I meet it
as a friend.

~ SYLVIA BOORSTEIN

Center Your Body

WEEK 41   DATE _____

1. Stand and feel your feet on the ground. Pour your attention into your right foot. Notice the points of pressure on the foot and the way your weight shifts. Then shift your concentration to your left foot. Are you able to feel both feet at the same time?

_____

_____

_____

2. Set a timer for 10 minutes. Sit comfortably. Where do you feel points of contact and tactile sensations where your body ends and the outside world begins?

_____

_____

_____

3. Begin by noticing your breath without changing it. For the next 5 to 10 minutes gently lengthen, deepen, and expand the breath. Don't force it. Relax and allow the breath to open naturally. How did that feel?

_____

_____

_____

4. How does your body feel when you're happy and having fun?

_____

_____

_____

5. Consider the space element. Observe the area around objects. Can you sense the space that exists within your body? Do you experience it directly or are you imagining it?

_____

_____

_____

6. Be still and notice your body. Where do you feel stuck or numb?

_____

_____

_____

7. Stand upright, pause, and relax. Notice the weight distribution of your feet. Feel the connection between your feet, legs, pelvis, spine, shoulders, and skull. What did you notice?

_____

_____

_____

Explore Your Mind

WEEK 42   DATE_____

1. Think of an ordinary task that you avoid because you don't like doing it. What happens in your mind? Can you sense tension just by thinking about this activity?

_____

_____

_____

_____

2. **LOOK BACK** to the first few weeks of this journal. Notice your increased ability to be mindful and how noticing this nourishes you. Reflect on how far you've come.

_____

_____

_____

_____

3. A part of mindfulness is observing when unwholesome mind states are not present. Next time you're feeling happy or content, observe how feelings of anger or greed are not arising. What's it like to notice?

_____

_____

_____

_____

4. Think of something you're sad about. Let it be. Our reaction usually makes pain worse. For now, can you allow and embrace sadness as if it's a small child in need of attention?

_____

_____

_____

5. Set a timer for 10 minutes. Relax, close your eyes, accept what is here, and notice thoughts. Take a mental note when thoughts are about the future and the past. What did you discover?

_____

_____

_____

6. Set a timer for five minutes. Relax with your eyes softly open. Notice the impermanent nature of all things. Sensations, thoughts, feelings all appear and disappear. What remains?

_____

_____

_____

7. What is the overall tone of your thinking right now? Is there something on your mind?

_____

_____

_____

WEEK 43   DATE_____

1. What is one supportive thing you can do for a friend this week?

_____

_____

_____

_____

2. Equanimity is an important aspect of mindfulness and self-care. We may wish ourselves and others continuous wellness, but struggle is a natural part of life. Can you think of a person or situation that you want to be different in some way, but you don't have control over the outcome?

_____

_____

_____

_____

3. Find time today to take a short nap. Turn the lights off, snuggle up, and doze off. Revel in this time of rest and letting go. How did that feel?

_____

_____

_____

_____

4. Close your eyes and loosen any analysis of your experience. Tend to your heart. What does your heart need right now?

_____

_____

_____

5. Go outside and touch a tree you feel connected to. Imagine the tree absorbing your anger, stress, and fatigue. Aim to let go. How do you feel now?

_____

_____

_____

6. Bring to mind a person you have deep care for. It could be someone you love or a child. Completely feel compassion for this being. How is it to recognize you can care so deeply?

_____

_____

_____

7. As we become more mindful, we see what truly makes us happy. **LOOK BACK** to the exercises in weeks 12, 20, and 28. Do you see any patterns? What truly makes you happy today?

_____

_____

_____

Celebrate & Appreciate

WEEK 44   DATE_____

1. How can you celebrate and appreciate yourself this week?

_____
_____
_____

2. What are some reasons you like your work today?

_____
_____
_____

3. Call to mind an object you own that has an important history. Consider all that occurred for the object to now be in your possession. What item did you choose? Why?

_____
_____
_____

4. What is one thing you like about your life right now?

_____
_____
_____
_____

5. Recall a specific time when you were sick and someone cared for you. Welcome a feeling of gratitude into your body, heart, and mind. How did this person help you?

_____

_____

_____

_____

6. What is one quality you possess that makes you a good person?

_____

_____

_____

_____

7. Even amid darkness there is light. Think back to a time when you were having a hard time. Was there a person or moment that seemed to be your shining light?

_____

_____

_____

_____

_____

_____

_____

Deep happiness doesn't come from gaining status or getting more stuff. True happiness is rooted in letting go and changing where we seek happiness. One way we can build happiness is through generosity. List three people you can give to or do something for, however small, this coming week.

*

*

*

The critical moment of the path, which breaks open the loving heart, is the realization that we have never existed as separate, isolated beings. When wisdom recognizes our oneness and sees the interconnectedness of all beings, it fills us with a degree of happiness that transforms our lives.

~ SHARON SALZBERG

Center Your Body

WEEK 45   DATE _____

1. When our digestive system is working optimally, we often feel better in our bodies. When we feel better in our bodies, we're able to be more present in our lives. Plan out a few meals in the space that follows.

_____

_____

_____

2. Go outside and pay attention to all five elements in nature: earth, water, fire, air, and space. Feel and appreciate their unique qualities.

_____

_____

_____

3. Lie on your back and relax. Stretching your body while lying down can be very restful. Reach and stretch your arms and legs out several times. Modify the movement to suit your needs. What did you notice?

_____

_____

_____

_____

4. Relax the tension in your body. Feel air entering and exiting your nostrils for at least 10 breaths. Don't let your attention wander. What's the difference between the inhale and the exhale?

_____

_____

_____

5. How does your body feel when you're content?

_____

_____

_____

6. What would support your body right now?

_____

_____

_____

7. Stand up and shift your weight to one foot. As you balance, notice reactivity. Are you holding your breath? Tensing your body? What happens in your mind?

_____

_____

_____

_____

Explore Your Mind

WEEK 46   DATE_____

1. Take a moment to notice if your face feels tense. Soften your tongue and turn the corners of your mouth up. Feel any facial tension surrender. As you release your face does your mind also relax?

_____

_____

_____

2. LOOK BACK to week 33 #6. Do the practice again and this time notice if your mind wants to label one side good or bad. Does your mind want to interpret or try to fix the side it deems incorrect?

_____

_____

_____

3. Sit quietly. Think about how you approach your life: Is it with a sense of trust or a need to control? Are there ways in which you try to control or manipulate your life when it would be easier to trust and let go?

_____

_____

_____

4. Sit and watch thoughts, feelings, sounds, and emotions rise and fall. When your mind grabs ahold of a particular thought, relax and lightly ask yourself: Who is thinking? Who is aware?

---

5. In conversation with a friend or loved one, discuss something you've learned about yourself from these mindfulness practices. What did you discuss?

---

6. LOOK BACK to "Practice" after week 44. Do you remember your state of mind when you were contemplating giving? Reflect below.

---

7. When do you feel most connected to a sense of peace? When does peace seem the furthest away? What conditions need to be present for you to find peace?

Take Care

WEEK 47   DATE _____

1. LOOK BACK to week 43 #2. How could you practice acceptance of this situation?

_____

_____

_____

2. Open the windows in your house today and let some fresh air in. How do you feel now?

_____

_____

_____

3. We can enforce states of mind such as calm, contentment, and happiness by being mindful of factors that stimulate ill will. What circumstances cause you to react from a place of ill will versus kindness?

_____

_____

_____

4. Choose one grounding word for today.

_____

5. Think of someone who is naturally radiant and happy. It could be someone you know or someone whom you look up to that you haven't met personally. Reflect on their good energy and simply delight in the joy of this person. Who did you choose? Why?

_____

_____

_____

_____

6. Actively look for positive events today. Let good news and small positive moments in daily life really impact you. Be mindful and feel each event fully for at least 10 seconds. How did it go?

_____

_____

_____

_____

7. Remember a time when you felt wronged by someone. Take note of how you reacted. Consider the endless causes and conditions that led to that moment. Acknowledge this person's history, pain, or beliefs. Do you feel differently about them now?

_____

_____

_____

_____

Faced with all your thoughts, feelings, and struggles, it's normal to sometimes feel lonely or disheartened. When confronted with the task of seeing yourself clearly, remind yourself that there are so many others just like you who are practicing diligently toward a more mindful life. You're not alone.

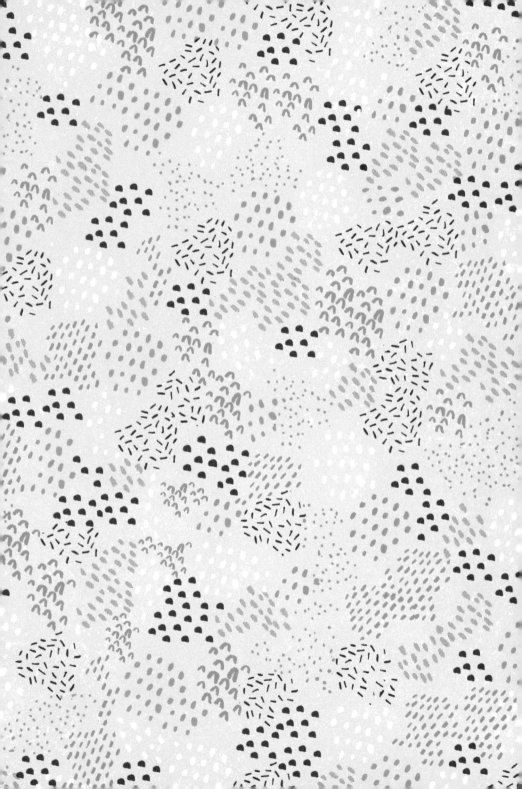

Celebrate & Appreciate

WEEK 48   DATE_____

1. How can you celebrate and appreciate someone you love this week?

_____

_____

_____

_____

2. Think back to your evolution and development as a human being. Describe an earlier self and three ways you have grown into a better person.

_____

_____

_____

_____

3. If you could create a life you love what would it be like?

_____

_____

_____

_____

_____

_____

4. There are many other people, just like you, learning mindfulness, trying to be a better person, and aiming to lead a kinder more compassionate life. How does it feel to recognize that?

_____

_____

_____

_____

_____

5. Choose one encouraging word for today.

_____

6. Next time you have a meal, think about the energy the meal provides. Cherish the energy and food. How did that feel?

_____

_____

_____

_____

_____

7. What is one skill you have that you're grateful for?

_____

_____

_____

_____

Think of a cherished friend of yours. What are the qualities they possess that make them so significant? Are they funny, caring, or trustworthy? Have they been there when you needed them? Write a letter below telling them how much they mean to you and why.

THIS IS ALWAYS THE MEASURE OF MINDFUL
PRACTICE—WHETHER WE CAN CREATE
THE CONDITIONS FOR LOVE AND PEACE IN
CIRCUMSTANCES THAT ARE DIFFICULT, WHETHER
WE CAN STOP RESISTING AND SURRENDER,
WORKING WITH WHAT WE HAVE, WHERE WE ARE.

~ bell hooks

Center Your Body

WEEK 49   DATE_____

1. Set a timer for 15 minutes. Sit comfortably and bring your attention to the center of your body. Feel your spine from your tailbone to the base of your skull. Stay present. Describe your experience.

_____

_____

_____

_____

2. Set a timer for 10 minutes. Sit quietly and sense your heartbeat. Place your fingers on your wrist or neck and sense the movement of blood, then release. Can you still feel your pulse?

_____

_____

_____

_____

3. LOOK BACK to week 13 #6, week 17 #5, week 21 #6, week 37 #1, and week 41 #6 to remember the elements. Ask yourself: Is there anything that doesn't fit into earth, water, fire, air, and space?

_____

_____

_____

_____

4. What is your relationship to your body right now? Is it cooperative or antagonistic?

_____

_____

_____

5. Sit, settle, relax, and breathe for 15 minutes. Imagine your body is still and strong like an ancient mountain. Let the waters of thought and the winds of feeling move around you without being swayed. Do you feel the strong, stable support in your body?

_____

_____

_____

6. What do you notice in your body today?

_____

_____

_____

7. Breathe slowly through your nose. After your next exhale, pause and hold before taking another breath. Repeat several times. If you feel stressed in any way, return to your regular breath. How do you feel now?

_____

_____

_____

Explore Your Mind

WEEK 50

DATE_____

1. Focus your awareness on your body. Slowly move your attention from your head down to your toes. Aim to keep your mind steady and concentrated as you migrate your focus. What was that like?

_____

_____

_____

2. In formal mindfulness practice, practitioners sometimes renounce complexity in favor of simplicity. This helps enhance clarity of mind. How could you simplify your life to support mindfulness?

_____

_____

_____

3. Mindfulness denies nothing. Instead, we see what is there, and work to understand its true nature, causes, and conditions. Is there a mind state you've been rejecting? Why have you been denying it?

_____

_____

_____

_____

4. Take some time today for conscious relaxation. Lie down, soften your body, and quiet your mind for 15 minutes. Invite your breath to be natural. Can you rest without falling asleep?

_____

_____

_____

5. Take a few moments to enjoy a glass of water. Intentionally slow down and immerse yourself in the experience. Ask yourself: Who is drinking this water?

_____

_____

_____

6. Sit and relax for 15 minutes. Call to mind a circumstance in your life that is currently triggering difficult feelings. Then, imagine you are somehow separate from this trigger. How do you experience yourself now?

_____

_____

_____

7. How can you cultivate more calm in your life today?

_____

_____

_____

Take Care

WEEK 51

1. Think of a situation you simply can't control. Offer yourself, or others involved, a few minutes of silent affirmation. Repeat: "May I accept things as they are," while focusing on cultivating equanimity. How do you feel?

_____

_____

_____

2. Relax and be present for the next 10 minutes. Draw your attention to a time or place you felt safe. Vividly remember as many details as you can. Rest in that feeling of safety. What do you remember?

_____

_____

_____

3. Consider someone who is suffering. Practice compassion by connecting with your own experience of hardship. Feel your heartfelt desire for this person to be well. Practice acceptance for how things are right now. Reflect.

_____

_____

_____

_____

4. Turn on your favorite music and simply listen. Enjoy mindfully without any other distractions. What did you listen to?

_____

_____

_____

5. Is there something you know you need to do that you've been putting off? What is it? How can you make a plan to accomplish it soon?

_____

_____

_____

6. Think of being with a person who really cares for you. Receive a feeling of love, warmth, and security. Let it enter your body, heart, and mind. Describe your experience.

_____

_____

_____

7. Add some flowers to your home today. Enjoy their scent and natural beauty. What kind of flowers did you choose?

_____

_____

_____

Celebrate & Appreciate

WEEK 52   DATE_____

1. Send a message to someone you appreciate today. Tell them how you feel and why you're grateful for their presence. Who did you choose? Why?

_____

_____

_____

2. Write a list of five people who have taught you something meaningful. What did they teach you?

_____

_____

_____

_____

3. Much of life centers around talking, reading, and acting constantly. The practice of deliberate silence invites deeper awareness. What would it be like to rest in silence and stop "doing" for a whole day?

_____

_____

_____

4. Take a few photos today of the things you're grateful for. Aim to be mindful and present while taking the photos. What images did you capture?

_____

_____

_____

5. How can you celebrate and appreciate a person who is having a hard time this week?

_____

_____

_____

6. Throughout your mindfulness trek using this journal, you've probably gained some insight into what you value. What have you discovered? Write three personal statements you wish to live by moving forward.

_____

_____

_____

7. What are three things you've learned from the mindfulness practices in this journal?

_____

_____

_____

This coming week create a vision of what is possible. Expand into a more positive expression of yourself! Tap into your creativity and imagine what life would be like if you cultivated a positive outlook on a regular basis.

When you love someone, the best thing you can offer is your presence. How can you love if you are not there?

~ THICH NHAT HANH

Resources

Many of the practices in this journal are the result of years of study with many skilled teachers. I'm deeply grateful to those who have influenced my study of this ancient practice. To learn more about mindfulness, please enjoy the following resources.

Websites

Dharmaseed. https://dharmaseed.org/
Mindful Yin Yoga Online. https://mindfulyinyoga.com/
Mindfulness Resources. https://jenniferraye.com/mindfulness
Spirit Rock Meditation Center. https://www.spiritrock.org/

Books

Brach, Tara. *Radical Acceptance: Embracing Your Life with the Heart of a Buddha.* New York: Bantam Books, 2003.

Cushman, Anne. *Moving into Meditation: A 12-Week Mindfulness Program for Yoga Practitioners.* Boston: Shambhala, 2014.

Farhi, Donna. *The Breathing Book: Good Health and Vitality Through Essential Breath Work.* New York: St. Martin's Griffin, 1996.

Goldstein, Joseph. *Mindfulness: A Practical Guide to Awakening.* Boulder, CO: Sounds True, 2013.

Gunaratana, Bhante Henepola. *Mindfulness in Plain English.* Boston: Wisdom Publications, 2002.

Hanson, Rick. *Buddha's Brain: The Practical Neuroscience of Happiness, Love, and Wisdom.* Oakland, CA: New Harbinger Publications, 2009.

Kornfield, Jack. *A Path with Heart: A Guide Through the Perils and Promises of Spiritual Life.* New York: Bantam Books, 1993.

Little, Tias. *Yoga of the Subtle Body: A Guide to the Physical and Energetic Anatomy of Yoga.* Boulder, CO: Shambhala, 2016.

Salzberg, Sharon. *Loving-kindness: The Revolutionary Art of Happiness.* Boston: Shambhala, 1995.

Wallace, B. Alan. *Genuine Happiness: Meditation as the Path to Fulfillment.* Hoboken, NJ: John Wiley & Sons, 2005.

References

Barks, Coleman. *The Essential Rumi.* New York: Harper Collins, 1995.

Boorstein, Sylvia. *Happiness Is an Inside Job: Practicing for a Joyful Life.* New York: Ballantine Books, 2008.

Brach, Tara. *Radical Acceptance: Embracing Your Life with the Heart of a Buddha.* New York: Bantam Books, 2003.

Brown, Brené. *Daring Greatly: How the Courage to Be Vulnerable Transforms the Way We Live, Love, Parent, and Lead.* New York: Avery, 2012.

Campbell, Joseph. *The Power of Myth.* New York: Anchor, 1991.

Chödrön, Pema. *Comfortable with Uncertainty: 108 Teachings on Cultivating Fearlessness and Compassion.* Boston: Shambhala, 2002.

Cushman, Anne. *Moving into Meditation: A 12-Week Mindfulness Program for Yoga Practitioners.* Boston: Shambhala, 2014.

Farhi, Donna. *The Breathing Book: Good Health and Vitality Through Essential Breath Work.* New York: St. Martin's Griffin, 1996.

Goldstein, Joseph. *Mindfulness: A Practical Guide to Awakening.* Boulder: Sounds True, 2013.

Gunaratana, Bhante Henepola. *Mindfulness in Plain English.* Boston: Wisdom Publications, 2002.

Hanh, Thich Nhat. *No Death, No Fear: Comforting Wisdom for Life.* New York: Riverhead Books, 2002.

Hanson, Rick. *Buddha's Brain: The Practical Neuroscience of Happiness, Love, and Wisdom.* Oakland, CA: New Harbinger Publications, 2009.

hooks, bell. *The Best Buddhist Writing 2007.* Edited by Melvin McCleod. Boston: Shambhala Publications, 2007.

Kornfield, Jack. *A Path with Heart: A Guide Through the Perils and Promises of Spiritual Life.* New York: Bantam Books, 1993.

Kimmerer, Robin Wall. *Braiding Sweetgrass: Indigenous Wisdom, Scientific Knowledge, and the Teachings of Plants.* Minneapolis, MN: Milkweed Editions, 2013.

Mother Teresa Quotes. BrainyQuote.com, BrainyMedia Inc, 2019. Accessed June 26, 2019. https://www.brainyquote.com/quotes/mother_teresa_121373.

Oliver, Mary. *Upstream.* New York: Penguin Press, 2016.

Salzberg, Sharon. *Loving-kindness: The Revolutionary Art of Happiness.* Boston: Shambhala, 1995.

Wallace, B. Alan. *Genuine Happiness: Meditation as the Path to Fulfillment.* Hoboken, NJ: John Wiley & Sons, 2005.

About the Author

Jennifer Raye holds her doctorate in Traditional Chinese Medicine. She is a licensed acupuncturist, herbalist, holistic nutritionist, mindfulness meditation teacher, and an experienced yoga and movement teacher.

Influenced and supported by her years of formal study and personal practice, Jennifer's offerings reflect her extensive and varied expertise in the fields of contemplative practice and integrative medicine. Steeped in the wisdom of the Buddha Dharma, and her deep respect for the beauty and magic of the natural world, her teachings emphasize self-care, and are holistic and therapeutic.

Jennifer teaches classes, retreats, and teacher training, locally and internationally, in addition to running her private medical practice. She is also the creator of a number of online programs. For more information and free resources visit www.jenniferraye.com.

Jennifer lives with her husband on Vancouver Island, Canada. She loves writing, traveling, dancing, growing food in her garden, and swimming in the rivers and lakes near her home.